Anteaters

Anteaters

Melissa Gish

Living Wild

CREATIVE EDUCATION

CREATIVE PAPERBACKS

Published by Creative Education and Creative Paperbacks
P.O. Box 227, Mankato, Minnesota 56002
Creative Education and Creative Paperbacks are imprints
of The Creative Company
www.thecreativecompany.us

Book design by Tom Morgan (www.bluedes.com)
Art direction by Rita Marshall
Book production by Ciara Beitlich
Edited by Joe Tischler

Photographs by Dreamstime (Lukyslukys), Flickr (James Basire/Bio
Diversity Heritage Library, Bio Diversity Heritage Library, Alfred Edmund
Brehm/Bio Diversity Heritage Library, Lydie, Zoological Society of
London, Getty (Peter Chadwick, Westend61), iStock (belizar73, CraigRJD,
dbvirago, hugocorzo, JordL, Kung Mangkorn, Saddako, Sand1983),
Shutterstock (Uwe Bergwitz, Matthieu Gallet, GR92100, Leonardo
Mercon, Martin Pelanek, Olena Znak), Wikimedia Commons (inaturalist,
Katja Schulz/Flickr, Quartl, Quinten Questel, Wellcome Library London)

Library of Congress Cataloging-in-Publication Data
Names: Gish, Melissa, author.
Title: Anteaters / Melissa Gish.
Description: Mankato, Minnesota : Creative Education and Creative
    Paperbacks, [2024] | Series: Living wild | Includes bibliographical
    references and index. | Audience: Ages 10–14 | Audience:
    Grades 7–9 | Summary: "Brimming with photos and
    scientific facts, this middle-grade nonfiction book about
    anteaters treats researchers and wild animal lovers to a
    comprehensive zoological profile of these long-tongued mammals.
    Includes sidebars, a range map, a glossary, and an Amazonian folktale
    about the anteater"— Provided by publisher.
Identifiers: LCCN 2023013191 (print) | LCCN 2023013192 (ebook) |
    ISBN 9781640267701 (library binding) | ISBN 9781682773208
    (paperback) | ISBN 9781640009400 (pdf)
Subjects: LCSH: Myrmecophagidae—Juvenile literature. | CYAC:
    Anteaters.
Classification: LCC QL737.E24 G573 2024 (print) | LCC QL737.E24
    (ebook) | DDC 599.3/14—dc23/eng/20230417
LC record available at https://lccn.loc.gov/2023013191
LC ebook record available at https://lccn.loc.gov/2023013192

Printed in China

CONTENTS

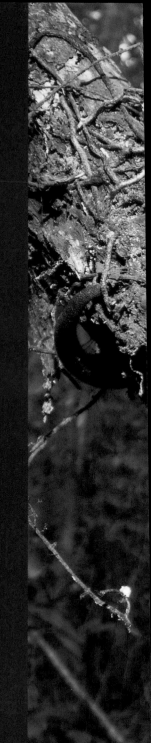

Asouthern tamandua slowly makes her way across the damp floor of Brazil's Amazon rainforest. Her month-old offspring, a miniature version of herself, clings to her back. The tamandua has discovered an ant nest. Caring for her young has given her a tremendous appetite. But the mother knows that the ants will attack as soon as she disturbs the nest. She needs to keep her baby safe from the danger. She climbs a nearby tree and selects a sturdy branch. Here she sets her offspring down. Sleepily, the baby tamandua grips the branch and nods off. Back on the ground, the mother goes to work. Her sharp claws tear into the nest. Her tongue moves with lightning speed, lapping up hundreds of ants in a matter of minutes. Satisfied with her snack, the tamandua shakes off the attacking ants and then climbs the tree to retrieve her youngster.

Anteaters typically avoid fire ants, which have venomous stings, and army ants, which have powerful bites.

Amazing Anteaters

With tube-shaped snouts, bushy tails, and long tongues that look like slender, slippery ropes, anteaters are some of the oddest animals on the planet.

Anteaters are insectivores, or animals that specialize in eating insects. They are found largely in Central and South America, where some live high in the rainforest **canopy**, and others roam the grasslands. Anteaters are members of the suborder Vermilingua, which comes from the Latin *vermis*, meaning "worm," and *lingua*, meaning "tongue." Anteaters and their closest relatives, sloths and armadillos, are mammals classified in the superorder Xenarthra (*zee-NARTH-ra*), also from Latin, meaning "strange joints." Xenarthrans have extra joints in their backbones, and unlike other mammals, they are not able to rotate their hips.

The largest anteater species is also the most at risk of **extinction**. The giant anteater can be found on savannas and grasslands from Honduras to southern Brazil and northern Argentina. It is diurnal, meaning it is most active during the day. Its brownish-gray fur is long, thick, and coarse—almost like straw—with a distinct pattern of black and gray stripes on its body and legs. From snout to tail, the giant anteater can be up to 7 feet (2.1 meters) long, and it can weigh more than 100 pounds (45 kilograms). Silky anteaters, the smallest anteaters, are **adapted** to an arboreal (tree-based) lifestyle. They range from southern Mexico throughout most of Central America and as far south as central Brazil. They also live on the island of Trinidad. Unlike their giant cousin, these anteaters are nocturnal, or active at night. They grow no longer than 18 inches (46 centimeters) and weigh less than 1 pound (0.5 kg). Their brownish-yellow fur is short, fine, and soft. Their faces are much shorter than other anteaters, and the underside of their **prehensile** tails are furless. There are seven recognized silky anteater species, but all are similar in appearance.

The two other anteater species are called tamanduas. The northern tamandua inhabits rainforests, cloud (or fog) forests, and mangrove swamps from southern Mexico to northwestern Venezuela and Peru, as well as offshore islands. The southern tamandua has a much larger range. It can be found on various islands, including Trinidad, and in forests, swamps, and savannas from Venezuela to northern Argentina and Uruguay. Tamanduas forage for food both on the ground and in trees. Each species has four subspecies based on geographical location. The subspecies vary greatly. They range in size from 28 to 61 inches (71–155 cm) from snout to tail, and their fur can be

Thanks to their small size, silky anteaters are also known as pygmy anteaters.

1. Northern Tamandua: southern Mexico, Central America, and coastal regions of Venezuela, Colombia, and Ecuador

2. Southern Tamandua: northern and central regions of South America

1

4

3   1

4   1   2

3

4   4

2

4

2

3   2

4. Silky Anteater: southern Mexico, Central America, and northern South America

3

3. Giant Anteater: southern Central America through southern Brazil and northern Argentina

Where in the World They Live

Anteaters inhabit forests and savannas of southern Mexico, Central America, and northern South America. Though widespread, the giant anteater's population is decreasing at an alarming rate. It is one of the most threatened mammals in Central America. As humans continue to encroach on and destroy anteater habitats, the animals' populations will continue to decline. The numbers on the map represent the areas in which each anteater can be found in the wild today.

The back of an anteater's tongue is attached to the breastbone and rolls up in the back of the anteater's skull.

creamy white to gold with dark markings on the torso and back. The markings vary by subspecies. Some tamanduas have brown stripes on their backs, while others appear to be wearing dark vests. Their fur is dense and coarse like the giant anteater's, but they have furless prehensile tails—similar to the silky anteater. The name "tamandua" derives from two words, *taa* (meaning "ant") and *mandeu* (meaning "trap"), in the language of the Tupi, an **indigenous** people of Brazil.

Anteaters feed on ants, termites, beetle **larvae**, and bees. They sometimes supplement their diet with fruit. The giant anteater laps up soft fruit that falls to the ground, while the other anteater species feed on fruit in the trees. They may also consume honey dripping from beehives. Anteaters' jaws are fused together. Only the tip of the mouth can open. Anteaters have no teeth. They rely on their tongue to capture prey. The giant anteater's tongue can be 24 inches (61 cm) long, tamanduas' tongues can be 16 inches (41 cm) long, and silky anteaters' are shorter still. The tongue has many small backward-facing spikes called papillae and is covered with sticky saliva produced by **glands** in the neck. The anteater flicks its tongue up to 150 times per minute, grabbing food and drawing it into the mouth, where it is swallowed whole. Unlike other mammals, which produce stomach acid to break down food, the anteater relies on the acid produced by the prey it eats. Ants and termites produce formic acid, which works like digestive juices in the anteater's stomach. In addition, anteaters often swallow sand and pebbles along with the insects. This debris helps crush food in their stomach.

Anteaters have five clawed toes on each hind foot. Giant anteaters have five front toes. Arboreal anteaters have four front toes. In all anteaters, two of the front toes have longer, curved claws suited to ripping into ant nests and termite mounds. These claws can be up to 4 inches (10 cm) long in the larger species. The claws are also used for defense. If threatened, a giant anteater will stand up on its back legs, using its tail for balance, and slash attackers with its front claws. Giant anteaters can walk with their back feet flat on the ground because their back claws are short, but they must curl their long front claws into a fist. Giant anteaters walk on their front knuckles, and tamanduas walk on the outsides of their front feet. Arboreal anteaters also use their claws to climb trees.

Anteaters have poor eyesight, but their sense of smell is 40 times better than a human's. When they find a food source, they use their claws to rip a hole in the nest or mound. Giant anteaters can consume 30,000 insects per day. Tamanduas consume up to 10,000 a day, and silky anteaters eat about 5,000. The

Silky anteaters have overlapping ribs that form a complete armored casing around their internal organs.

The thickest part of an anteater's tongue is the strongest, while the narrow end is more sensitive to touch.

animal's dense fur protects it from bites and stings as it rips into a nest. Anteaters never eat more than about 1 percent of the insects in a nest, and they never destroy a nest—they spend only a few minutes there before moving on. This ensures that the insect colony can survive and rebuild itself to provide the anteater with food on another day. Most anteaters are good swimmers, though they don't drink water. They get all the moisture they need from their food. The silky anteater is an exception. Remaining in the trees, it may lap dew from leaves and flowers.

Quick Meals and Power Naps

Anteaters are solitary animals that stay within an established area called a home range. The size of the home range depends on available resources and the number of anteaters in a given area.

In Brazil, where most giant anteaters live, home ranges are typically 1.4 to 3.5 square miles (3.6–9.1 square kilometers). In Venezuela, where fewer giant anteaters exist, home ranges can be as large as 9.5 square miles (25 sq km). Southern tamanduas may inhabit up to 1.4 square miles (3.6 sq km), while northern tamanduas and silky anteaters have territories no bigger than one-third of a square mile (0.8 sq km).

Female anteaters' home ranges often overlap, though individuals typically avoid each other. Males may challenge each other for territory. First, the males circle each other, making loud exhaling sounds, and then they try to chase each other away. If neither backs down, the anteaters may slash at each other with their sharp front claws or grab each other and wrestle until one gives up and goes away. Male and female anteaters come together only to mate.

Anteaters patrol the borders of their home ranges, leaving scent marks on trees. They use their powerful sense of smell to tell when nearby anteaters are ready to mate. There is no specific breeding season, but silky anteaters typically breed from

Anteaters leave their scent on trees using saliva and urine and by scratching the bark.

Young anteaters are nearly the same size as their mothers by the time they stop relying on her for food and protection.

December to February, while other anteaters usually breed from March to June. Little is known about anteater courtship. When a male anteater selects a female, he holds her down on her side to mate with her. Giant anteaters and tamanduas stay together for about three days, feeding from the same food sources and mating several times. These anteaters go their separate ways after mating.

The **gestation** period for giant anteaters is about 190 days. The mother gives birth to a single offspring while standing up. Baby anteaters are called pups. Minutes after birth, the pup crawls up its mother's body and clings to her back. The pup looks like a miniature version of its mother and may be so well camouflaged that it appears invisible against its mother's coat.

Because male anteaters' reproductive organs are inside their bodies, for hundreds of years, people thought all anteaters were female.

It will continue to ride on her back for up to a year, getting down only to feed. At first, it drinks the milk its mother produces. Later, it laps up partially digested insects that its mother regurgitates. The young anteater will remain close to its mother, and she will defend it from predators using her sharp claws. Jaguars and other predatory cats prey on pups. The giant anteater pup will not feed on its own until it is about two years old. Then it will wander away from its mother to establish its own home range. The giant anteater's life span in the wild is not known, but the oldest female in captivity died at age 31, and the oldest male died at age 22. Both lived at the Santa Barbara Zoo in California.

As a marsupial, the numbat, or banded anteater, carries its offspring in a pouch on the mother's belly.

Tamanduas can adjust their gestation period from 130 to 190 days, depending on weather conditions and food resources. After mating, the female makes a nest of dry leaves in the cavity of a tree. She gives birth to a single pup, which she keeps in the nest for a time. With a solid coat of soft fur ranging from white to black, the newborn pup initially looks very different from its mother. The pup clings to its mother's back when she goes out foraging, though she may leave it safely on a nearby branch while she feeds. Tamanduas mature quickly and are completely **weaned** by about nine months old. They are ready to leave their mothers at one year of age.

The gestation period of silky anteaters is 120 to 150 days. The parents remain together to care for the single pup that is born in a tree cavity. At first, the pup is left alone in a nest of dry leaves for up to eight hours while the parents forage. Later, it rides on either its mother's or its father's back. The pup drinks its mother's milk and later feeds on regurgitated insects provided by both parents. Silky anteaters tend to inhabit silk cotton trees more than any other type of tree. Because their fluffy bodies look similar to the fibers that spill from the seedpods of this tree, they can more successfully hide from predators such as harpy eagles and spectacled owls. Young silky anteaters are fully weaned and ready for life on their own at one year old.

Northern tamanduas spend about half their time in trees, with a preference for hollow or rotting trunks.

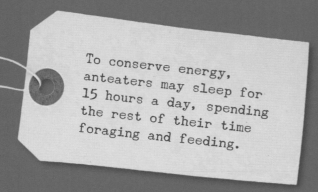

To conserve energy, anteaters may sleep for 15 hours a day, spending the rest of their time foraging and feeding.

Because giant anteaters are so much larger than tamanduas and silky anteaters, they must consume significantly more food each day than their smaller cousins. Despite their name, giant anteaters tend to eat more termites than ants when available. This is because termites have more protein pound-for-pound than any other food. In the anteater's habitat, termites eat dry grass and woody material. The termites ingest a fungus that grows inside this plant matter. The fungus provides more **nutrients** than the plant matter alone. In addition, special bacteria inside the termites' guts produce nitrogen, an important component in the production of protein. This **symbiotic** relationship among the termites, fungus, and bacteria provides giant anteaters with a nutrient-rich food source.

Because anteaters can feed for only about a minute before being attacked by their food source, they must constantly be on the move. Silky anteaters have been observed visiting 38 different trees and feeding on as many as 18 different ant species in a single night. But anteaters typically consume barely enough food to cover their energy needs. To conserve energy, anteaters maintain a low body temperature. In fact, anteaters have one of the lowest body temperatures of any mammal: 91 degrees Fahrenheit (33 degrees Celsius). They rest between meals, and while resting, they sometimes enter a state of torpor, a kind of temporary hibernation in which the body systems slow down. When giant anteaters sleep, they lie on their sides and wrap their bushy tails over their heads. When other anteaters sleep, they curl up in a ball in a tree cavity or on a leafy forked branch to conserve body heat.

For up to a year, anteater pups ride (and sometimes sleep) atop their parents' back.

Master of the Ants

Anteaters are important in the folklore and **mythology** of many Central and South American **cultures**. They are traditionally regarded either as enemies to be feared or valuable creatures to be revered.

Alessandra Bertassoni, a biologist at the Tamanduás Research and Conservation Institute of Brazil, published her research on the common beliefs and folklore surrounding giant anteaters in some rural Brazilian communities where giant anteaters are common. She discovered that people who make their living on farms and ranches often have a negative view of giant anteaters. Some of them believe that anteaters can suffocate dogs and people with their snouts and that anteaters symbolize bad luck, especially if they cross a person's path. The only safeguard is to kill the anteater and wear its claws as a charm to ward off evil.

Another belief held by farmers and ranchers is that anteaters are capable of killing jaguars and are dangerous to humans. In truth, jaguars regularly prey on anteaters. And though few

The shaggy hair on the giant anteater's tail can grow to be 16 inches (41 cm) long.

people have been killed by giant anteaters, researchers reported that, in every case, the animal was acting to protect itself. In one instance, a man was chasing an anteater with a machete because he believed it had killed and eaten some of his cattle. But anteaters are incapable of eating anything larger than a small beetle. Additionally, they are shy and tend to avoid humans and livestock. The myths depicting giant anteaters as dangerous predators are typically what lead to their conflict with humans. Scientists and conservationists want to educate people about anteaters because fear and misunderstanding of these animals—and the resulting persecution—could be contributing to the recent major decline in giant anteater populations.

In Brazil's rainforests, where many people live more traditional lifestyles, anteaters are typically viewed in a more positive light. The Kayapó are an indigenous people who live along the Xingu River in the eastern part of the Amazon rainforest. They have been in regular contact with nonnatives only since the 1960s, so their traditions remain very much alive. About 8,500 Kayapó live in 50 villages on protected land. They hunt and fish in traditional ways, wear traditional clothing and headdresses, and practice many rituals. One of their most important rituals is the name-giving ceremony. During this event, young people are given names based on their relationships with nature. Participants wear two types of costumes. One represents monkeys, which the people view as an important food source. (In fact, the people's name, *Kayapó*, means

Unlike pups of other anteater species, silky anteater pups are cared for by both parents.

"those who look like monkeys" and comes from this tradition of wearing monkey masks.) The other costume is the anteater. The tribe views ants as valuable members of the rainforest **ecosystem**. By breaking down leaf litter, ants help the forest grow, and the anteater is revered as the master of the ants.

The Bribrí people of southern Costa Rica have various superstitions relating to anteaters. One belief is that hanging the claws of a northern tamandua inside the home of a pregnant woman will give her child a strong, resilient spirit. The silky anteater is believed to be a divine creature that carries the Bribrí's souls to heaven. The Witoto, an indigenous people of southeastern

The 20th-century Spanish painter Salvador Dalí kept a pet giant anteater and occasionally walked it with a collar and leash.

Colombia and northern Peru, include the anteater in their creation myths. According to one story, the Father Spirit captured a mist and mixed it with soil. He spread this all around the world, and from it arose all the plants and animals, including the jaguar and the anteater, who could speak to each other in those early days and worked together to create the people.

In Trinidad, the silky anteater has the nickname "poor-me-one," which refers to the phrase "poor me, all alone." Long ago, people thought the silky anteater made a sorrowful, human-sounding cry in the forests at night. Later, it was discovered that a nocturnal bird, the common potoo, was responsible. Now both the bird and the silky anteater have the nickname. Anteaters have also had to share their name with other animals around the world—none of which is even related. In Africa, people often refer to the aardvark and the pangolin as anteaters. In Australia, the numbat is called the banded anteater, and the echidna is also known as the spiny anteater. These animals were called anteaters, no doubt, because they all have long snouts—though not nearly as long as true anteaters' snouts—and they all feed on insects, including ants.

Anteaters have proven to be popular characters in literature over the years. In Bernard Waber's classic 1967 book, *An Anteater Named Arthur*, the title character is a little anteater with a lot of questions about the world and a patient mother anteater who does her best to answer them. Carl Emerson's book *Nosy Arnie the Anteater* (2007) features a disrespected little anteater who proves his worth to his forest neighbors when he rescues a missing baby mouse. Gemma Raynor's 2014 book *Anthony and the Ants* describes a strange dispute between Anthony Anteater and the little insects that keep stealing his food. And in Karen Wallace's book *Ana Anteater Goes for Gold* (2016), a group of young anteaters set their sights on Olympic glory in the synchronized swimming competition.

A few countries made anteaters part of their national heritage by commemorating them on postage stamps. In 1904, French Guiana released a stamp featuring the giant anteater. This stamp was rereleased in 1922 and 1942, and in 1945, the country included the anteater in a stamp series of various animals on its **coats of arms**. In 1968, Honduras issued a colorful series of native wildlife stamps that included the northern tamandua. A year later, Paraguay celebrated the giant anteater on a stamp and also released an updated version in 1988. That same year, Brazil featured the giant anteater on its series of native animal stamps. Stamp collectors value anteater stamps because, like real-life anteaters, they appear quite infrequently.

Great Anteater

This animal is extremely rare in the Santa Marta mountains, though occasionally reported; the only one we heard of during our stay was seen by my son and two porters as they were passing on a mountain pass near Valparaiso, at an elevation of about 5,000 feet; they had no firearms, and as none of the party had ever seen the animal before, they hesitated to attack it with sticks; it moved down the mountainside and disappeared in the forest.

From the notes gathered in Brazil, it appears that the great anteater is essentially a forest animal, though sometimes coming out to the open lands; it eats insects and insect larvae of many kinds and, I believe, small fruits. The flesh is rarely eaten, and only in case of necessity.

— from *Bulletin of the American Museum of Natural History* (1904), by Herbert H. Smith (1851–1919)

Animal Tale: Silky Anteater's Trick

The people of the Amazon rainforest share their home with some of the planet's most unique wildlife. Their folklore is rich with tales about how these animals came to be. This traditional story from Brazil tells how the silky anteater got his claws.

One day, long ago, Anteater was walking in the forest, searching for something to eat. He heard a sound above him, so he looked up. There was Monkey, crunching on something.

"What are you eating?" Anteater called.

"I found a nest of delicious ladybugs," Monkey said, "but I cannot reach them all. They are deep inside this tree."

In those days, Monkey had stubby fingers, while Anteater had long, slender fingers that he used to reach deep into the nests of ants, beetles, and bees. "If you carry me up there," Anteater said, "I will help you."

"If I carry you up here, you will eat all the ladybugs yourself," said Monkey. "You should give me half of your long fingers, and then we will both feast."

Anteater was very hungry—and he especially loved fat, juicy ladybugs—so he agreed. Monkey scurried down the tree. He put Anteater on his back and clambered back up the tree. Then Anteater gave half of his long fingers to Monkey. Together they reached into the slim cracks in the tree and pulled out their fill of ladybugs.

"You may carry me down now," said Anteater.

"Of course," Monkey replied. But Monkey was a trickster. "I will carry you down," Monkey said, "if you give me the rest of your long fingers."

Anteater was shocked. "What do you mean?" he cried. "What will I use to collect insects?"

"Well," said the sneaky Monkey, "what good will your long fingers be when you are stuck in this tree for the rest of your life?"

Anteater looked down. It was an awfully long way to the forest floor. "Very well," he said. And with that, he gave Monkey the rest of his long fingers. Now he had only tiny stumps on his hands.

Just then, Jaguar appeared. Monkey was overcome with fear. He fled, leaving Anteater in the tree. *Oh no*, thought Anteater. *How will I ever get down now?* Then he had an idea. "Hello, Jaguar," he called. "Will you help me get down from this tree?"

Jaguar looked up and saw Anteater high above him. Everyone knows how much jaguars love to eat anteaters. A smile crept across Jaguar's face. "Well, of course," he replied, thinking how delicious Anteater would taste. "What can I do?" he asked.

"If you could toss me some of your claws," Anteater explained, "then I could climb down."

Jaguar had plenty of sharp, curved claws. And besides, he figured that he could take them back when he devoured Anteater. "Why, surely," Jaguar called. And with that, he tossed some of his claws up to Anteater.

With his new claws, Anteater was able to climb even higher in the tree. "Thank you," he called down to Jaguar, "but I think I will stay up here now." Jaguar loped away, feeling foolish that he had been tricked. And to this day, the silky anteater stays in the trees, safely out of the jaguar's reach, clawing his way into the nests of fat, juicy ladybugs.

Angels of the Forest

Anteater fossils are rare. Because of their solitary lifestyle and low population density, few of the animals were preserved as fossils.

The oldest direct ancestor of the giant anteater is believed to be *Neotamandua borealis*, which lived about 16 million years ago. Its remains were first discovered in the early 1970s at a fossil site called La Venta in Colombia. It was about half the size of modern giant anteaters and foraged both on the ground and in trees. About the same time that fossil was discovered, two amateur rock collectors were camping in Mexico's Sonoran Desert near El Golfo de Santa Clara when they happened upon the fossilized paw bone of a sharp-clawed mammal. They took the specimen to the Cincinnati Museum of Natural History.

The tiny fossil—just 2.5 inches (6.4 cm) long—was studied for 15 years before it was determined to be a bone from an early anteater that lived between 700,000 and 1 million years ago. This fossil is noteworthy because it was the first evidence of anteaters in North America. Scientists at the Natural History Museum of Los

 The University of California Irvine's athletic teams are one of the only college teams to have Anteaters as their nickname.

Giant anteaters eat mainly ants during rainy months and switch to mostly termites in dry months.

Giant anteaters tend to walk slowly, but if threatened, they can sprint short distances at up to 31 miles (50 km) per hour.

Angeles County, where the fossil resides today, believe that anteaters traveled north from South America to Mexico after the strip of land containing Panama emerged from underwater about three million years ago. These prehistoric anteaters were about the size of modern giant anteaters, so they required a lot of food. Some scientists think that during the last ice age (which lasted from about 110,000 to about 12,000 years ago), the shifting climate not only diminished the anteaters' food supply but also proved too cool for the anteaters themselves. This likely drove them back to Central and South America.

Even a couple of decades ago, giant anteaters were far more widespread than they are today. Only about 5,000 giant anteaters remain in the wild. Giant anteaters have been **extirpated** from their former ranges in Belize, El Salvador, Guatemala, Uruguay, and parts of Brazil, Ecuador, and Costa Rica. The International Union for Conservation of Nature (IUCN) lists the giant anteater as vulnerable. This means it is subject to a number of changes in its environment that hinder its ability to survive, particularly habitat destruction and deaths caused by fires and vehicle collisions. The IUCN estimates that the giant anteater population has been slashed by more than 30 percent since 1993.

Tennessee's Nashville Zoo is one organization that is working to conserve giant anteaters. The zoo is home to seven giant anteaters—the largest collection of captive giant anteaters in the United States. Research on giant anteater biology and reproduction has been ongoing since 2000, when the zoo received its first pair of giant anteaters from Guyana. Female giant anteaters do not show any outward signs of being pregnant, so the animals are closely monitored. Veterinarians analyze the females' **hormones** and monitor the development of pups inside mothers' bodies with ultrasonography. Ultrasound machines are similar to X-rays, but the technology uses sound waves to safely create a picture of something inside the body. Since 2001, 20 pups have been born at the zoo's breeding facility. After the young anteaters are weaned, they are sent to other zoos to provide **genetic** diversity in their breeding programs. The Netherlands's Artis Zoo and Zodiac Zoos, Argentina's Zoo de Florencio Varela, Spain's Barcelona Zoo, Germany's Dortmund Zoo, and France's Zoo de Doué-la-Fontaine are partners in another giant anteater conservation program.

Zoos are not the only agents of conservation. Individuals have been trying to make a difference as well. Since 2007, giant anteaters have been a major focus at Rincón del Socorro, located in the Iberá wetlands of northeastern Argentina. Giant anteaters had been absent from this region for many decades. But the owners of Rincón del Socorro decided to transform the roughly 30,000-acre (12,141 hectares) cattle ranch into an eco-resort and protected

nature reserve that would specialize in reintroducing giant anteaters to the Iberá wetlands. Their first two giant anteaters, named Ivoty Porá and Preto, settled in immediately. More were added, and soon the anteaters were breeding. Since 2008, anteaters in the reserve have given birth to more than 30 pups. Some of the anteaters were taken to a protected island in the Iberá wetlands called San Alonso. As of 2022, 23 anteaters inhabited the island.

Tamanduas and silky anteaters are not officially listed as endangered, but conservationists worry that their status could change soon. Scientists do not have even estimated populations for these species. Too little is known about them to fully appreciate the effects that urban development, deforestation, pollution, and climate change might have on these anteater species. In addition, anteaters are hunted for food and for the **tendons** in their tails, which are used to make rope. On the island of Trinidad, where most of the anteaters inhabit protected areas, **poaching** is widespread. In 2015, foresters and conservationists formed the Wildlife and Environmental Protection of Trinidad and Tobago (WEPTT), aiming to reduce poaching, promote sustainable hunting practices, and rescue and relocate wildlife that wander away from protected areas. The group is also pushing for stricter laws against the sale of wild animal meat.

The northern tamandua is also known as the vested tamandua because of its V-shaped "vest" of dark fur.

Though normally silent, tamanduas have been known to hiss when threatened or disturbed.

Giant anteaters are struggling, but dedicated researchers are working tirelessly to stay ahead of the threat of extinction. Other anteater species seem to be on their own for now. A first step toward recognizing what tree-dwelling anteaters need to survive is the ability to study them. But because these animals are so elusive, researching them in the wild is nearly impossible. In his 2003 book *Living on the Edge: Amazing Relationships in the Natural World*, conservationist Jeff Corwin wrote about seeing silky anteaters, confessing, "This mysterious, almost magical creature sends my heart aflutter each time I have the rare privilege to set my eyes upon it." Finding ways to understand and protect anteaters and their vital habitats is necessary if all anteater species are to survive into the future.

Glossary

adapt – a change to improve a species' chances of survival in its environment

canopy – the topmost leafy branches of |a forest

coat of arms – the official symbol of a family, state, nation, or other group

culture – a particular group in a society that shares behaviors and characteristics that are accepted as normal by the group

ecosystem – a community of organisms that live together in an environment

extinction – the act or process of becoming extinct; coming to an end or dying out

extirpate – to forcibly and completely remove or destroy

genetic – relating to genes, the basic physical units of heredity

gestation – the period of time it takes a baby to develop inside its mother's womb

gland – an organ in a human or animal body that produces chemical substances used by other parts of the body

hormone – a chemical substance produced in the body that controls and regulates the activity of certain cells and organs

indigenous – originating in a particular region or country

larva – the newly hatched, wingless, often wormlike form of many insects before they become adults

mythology – a collection of myths, or popular, traditional beliefs or stories that explain how something came to be or that are associated with a person or object

nutrient – a substance that gives a living thing energy and helps it grow

poach – to illegally hunt a protected species of wild animals

prehensile – capable of grasping

symbiotic – a kind of relationship between two or more living things that is good for all involved

tendon – a tough, inelastic tissue that connects muscle to bone

wean – to make the young of a mammal accept food other than nursing milk

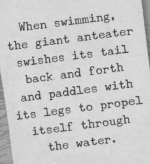

When swimming, the giant anteater swishes its tail back and forth and paddles with its legs to propel itself through the water.

Selected Bibliography

Animal Diversity Web. "Tamandua Mexicana: Northern Tamandua." http://animaldiversity.org/accounts/Tamandua_mexicana/.

Defler, Thomas. *History of Terrestrial Mammals in South America: How South American Mammalian Fauna Changed From the Mesozoic to Recent Times*. Cham: Springer International Publishing, 2019.

Macdonald, David W., ed. *The Princeton Encyclopedia of Mammals*. Princeton, N.J.: Princeton University Press, 2009.

San Diego Zoo Wildlife Alliance. "Giant Anteater." http://animals.sandiegozoo.org/animals/giant-anteater.

Smithsonian's National Zoo & Conservation Biology Institute. "Southern Tamandua." https://nationalzoo.si.edu/animals/southern-tamandua.

Spilsbury, Louise. *Animal Bodies: Extreme Anatomies*. New York: Gareth Stevens Publishing, 2015.

Index